OTHER BOOKS BY ALEX MITCHELL

Quizzin' Nine-Nine: A Brooklyn Nine-Nine Quiz Book
Parks & Interrogation: A Parks & Recreation Quiz Book
Q & AC-12: A Line of Duty Quiz Book
Know Your Schitt: A Schitt's Creek Quiz Book

Examilton

A Hamilton Musical Quiz Book

Published by Beartown Press

Copyright © 2020 Alex Mitchell

ISBN: 9798672052892

Contents

Introduction

Hamilton first entered my consciousness back in 2015 when my wife became obsessed with the soundtrack, seemingly out of nowhere.

Truthfully, I thought it would be a temporary phase. My wife has a habit of being attracted to things that are somewhat hit-and-miss. Myself, for example.

But her interest in both the musical and myself continued, and so it wasn't long before I accompanied her in a plus-one capacity to a West End production of Hamilton for her birthday.

That night I was bitten by the bug and fell in love with what I can only describe as a wonderful piece of theater from the mind of the sickeningly-talented Lin-Manuel Miranda.

There's little I can add to the superlatives and opinion already posted to the Hamilton pigeonhole by critics far more qualified than myself, except to say that it's the finest musical I've ever seen which features French rapping.

Thank you for picking up this book. Here's what you have on your hands:

- 400 quiz questions about the musical Hamilton.

- Questions are separated into 26 themed rounds, including a final set of tiebreakers to separate the Elizas from the E-losers.

- Answer sheets for each round are located in the second half.

- If you haven't actually seen Hamilton, please do be aware that this book contains spoilers (ish). Also, just put the book down and go and watch Hamilton instead.

- If you enjoy the book and feel like leaving a review for it, please do - it helps a lot.

However, if you're ready to go ahead and separate the Founding Fathers from the floundering fathers, let's go...

General Knowledge

1. What is the official subtitle of the Hamilton stage production, often appearing within its logo?

2. Which character introduces Hamilton and Eliza to one another?

3. Which character works to recruit an all-black military regiment?

4. What is the name (and song title) given to the document Hamilton writes to come clean about his affair in an attempt to save his political legacy?

5. Which king appears in Hamilton?

6. What is the only Hamilton song in which Hamilton and Burr harmonize?

7. What was Hercules Mulligan's occupation?

8. What was the name given to the collection of essays through which Hamilton and two others defended the new U.S. Constitution?

9. What is the surname of the general after whom Clermont Street is renamed, as related to Hamilton by Burr?

10. To the closest hundred, how much money did Hamilton pay to James Reynolds?

11. As shown in Hamilton, in which state does America's capital end up being held?

12. Eliza's first line in Hamilton describes Alexander's father leaving the family. How old was Alexander at the time?

13. What is the "drinking song" sung by the British as they retreat from Yorktown?

14. Who changes the rule that "the guy who comes in second gets to be Vice President"?

15. What is the final line of Hamilton?

Answers on page 67

Hamilton

1. How old was Hamilton when he was placed in charge of a trading charter?

2. To which educational facility does Hamilton proclaim he'll go on to receive a scholarship?

3. On which denomination of dollar bill can Hamilton's face now be found?

4. Who, according to the opening number, is Hamilton the son of?

5. Who is said to have named their feral tomcat after Hamilton?

6. Hamilton is said to grow up to be "a hero and a..." *what*?

7. How many essays did Hamilton personally write, as related in 'Non-Stop', in order to defend the new U.S. Constitution?

8. At the end of Act 1, Hamilton becomes Secretary of the Treasury in the Washington administration. Which other role is he expecting to be offered?

9. How many things does Hamilton announce that he hasn't done (but just you wait)?

10. Who does Hamilton describe as his first friend?

11. Which emergency service did Hamilton create, according to 'The Adams Administration'?

12. Hamilton tells Burr he first heard his name where?

13. Which "client" does Hamilton approach Burr, a better lawyer than him, to defend?

14. What is the name of Hamilton's second in his duel with Burr?

15. What is Alexander Hamilton's first line in Hamilton?

Answers on page 68

The Nerd Round

1. Who was the author of the book which inspired Lin-Manuel Miranda to write Hamilton (and also acted as a historical consultant on the off-Broadway production)?

2. What was the original title of Hamilton, when it was first performed as a working production?

3. At which theatre did Hamilton debut on Broadway?

4. Which is the longest song in Hamilton?

5. Which British actor gave Lin-Manuel Miranda the central line and title of 'You'll Be Back'?

6. And which actress/singer did Lin-Manuel Miranda write the music to 'Satisfied' for?

7. What is the name of the client defended by both Hamilton and Burr in "the first murder trial of our new nation"?

8. What is the name of the Hamilton song/scene which appears in the live production but which doesn't make it onto the cast album?

9. Which Hamilton song features a section that's the fastest-sung song on Broadway?

10. In which comedy series did Lin-Manuel Miranda appear in an extended supporting role, during which he took part in a Burr-Hamilton-style duel at a paintball range in the season finale?

11. Which other Hamilton role did Lin-Manuel Miranda consider playing?

12. What was 'Blow Us All Away' originally titled?

13. A number of roles are doubled between Act One and Two - Lafayette and Jefferson, for example. But which character does the role of James Reynolds double with?

14. According to Lin-Manual Miranda, the line "Here's an itemized list of thirty years of disagreements" line in 'Your Obedient Servant' is an homage to which American sitcom?

15. What is Alexander's final line in Hamilton?

<u>Answers on page 70</u>

The Ten Duel Commandments

Can you name the missing words from 'The Ten Duel Commandments'?

Number one.

1. "The challenge, demand _____."

2. "If they _____, no need for further action."

Number two.

3. "If they don't, grab a friend, that's your _____."

4. "Your _____ when there's reckoning to be reckoned."

Number three.

5. "Have your [answer to 3]s meet face-to-face. Negotiate a _____. Or negotiate a time and place."

6. "This is commonplace, 'specially 'tween recruits. Most disputes die, and no one _____."

Number four.

7. "If they don't reach a [answer to 5], that's alright. Time to get some _____ and a doctor on site."

8. "You pay him in advance, you treat him with civility. You have him turn around so he can have _____."

Five.

9. "Duel before the sun is in the sky. Pick a place to die where it's high and _____."

Number six.

10. "Leave a _____ for your next of kin. Tell 'em where you been."

11. "Pray that _____ or heaven lets you in."

Seven.

12. "Confess your sins. Ready for the moment of _____ when you finally face your opponent."

Number eight.

13. "Your last chance to_____. Send in your [answer to 3]s, see if they can set the record straight."

Number nine.

14. "Look 'em in the eye, aim no higher. Summon all the _____ you require. Then count. One two three four. Five six seven eight nine."

Number ten (paces).

15. "_____."

Answers on page 72

Eliza

1. What color does Eliza primarily wear in the stage production: yellow, green or pink?

2. In Hamilton, Eliza is a resident of which state?

3. How long after their first meeting is Eliza writing a letter to Hamilton "nightly"?

4. And in which part of New York does Hamilton tell Eliza that they'll "get a little place in... and figure it out"?

5. Which instrument does Eliza teach Philip to play?

6. What is the two-word advice given to Hamilton by Eliza's father, while he provides his blessing to marry Eliza?

7. According to Eliza, who spends the summer with his family?

8. Eliza writes to George Washington to request that he be sent home from the war as she is pregnant. But in which song does she tell Hamilton of her pregnancy?

9. What is the name of Eliza's father?

10. In which song does Eliza remove herself from the narrative?

11. And in which song does she put herself back into the narrative?

12. In which two categories does Hamilton describe Eliza as being the best of?

13. How long does Eliza say she lives for after Hamilton's death?

14. Which landmark in D.C. does Eliza raise funds for?

15. And what does Eliza establish the first ever of in New York City?

Answers on page 74

Act One

1. Who delivers the first line of Act One?

2. Lafayette describes himself as the *what* "of the revolutionary set"?

3. What beverage has John Laurens consumed two of (but he's working on three) in 'Aaron Burr, Sir'?

4. In 'My Shot', what distance ahead of him does Hamilton imagine death might be?

5. How many troops is British Admiral Howe said to have on the water in New York Harbor, in 'Right Hand Man'?

6. What does Hamilton go to steal from the British in 'Right Hand Man'?

7. In the opening number, which two characters say "We fought with him"?

8. Who does Washington promote to general ahead of Hamilton, much to the latter's consternation?

9. What does Hamilton write to Congress that the army has resorted to eating?

10. In 'A Winter's Ball', Burr describes one thing that he and Hamilton have in common - what is it?

11. In which state does John Laurens die (ending up there after being "scattered to the winds" with the rest of Hamilton's friends)?

12. Which two people, along with Hamilton, contributed to the anonymous series of essays defending the new U.S. Constitution?

13. In 'Yorktown', what is the code word?

14. When the Americans finally drive the British away, where is Lafayette waiting?

15. What is the final song of Act One?

Answers on page 76

Follow That Line

Can you remember the line that follows these Hamilton lyrics?

1. "If you stand for nothing, Burr..."

2. "Grab my sister, and whisper..."

3. "Hey yo, I'm just like my country..."

4. "Oceans rise, empires fall. Next to Washington..."

5. "Insane, your family brings out a different side of me. Peggy confides in me..."

6. "I will send a fully armed battalion..."

7. "Angelica tell my wife..."

8. "This is commonplace 'specially 'tween recruits..."

9. "At least my dear Eliza's his wife..."

10. "Death doesn't discriminate..."

11. "Dear Theodosia, what to say to you? You have my eyes..."

12. "And when I meet Thomas Jefferson, I'm 'a compel him to..."

13. "Should we honor our treaty, King Louis's head?"

14. "Two Virginians and an immigrant walk into a room..."

15. "If there's a fire you're trying to douse..."

Answers on page 78

Angelica

1. What color does Angelica primarily wear in the stage production: yellow, green or pink?

2. Which book does Angelica announce she has been reading, in 'The Schuyler Sisters'?

3. What does Angelica tell Eliza she is looking for, in 'The Schuyler Sisters'?

4. In the same song, what does Burr tell Angelica her perfume smells like?

5. Which Shakespeare play do Angelica and Hamilton reference in their letters to one another?

6. Which word does Angelica use to describe the gossip in New York City?

7. In the stage production, who does Hamilton stop from approaching Angelica before they speak for the first time at the winter ball?

8. In 'Satisfied', what does Angelica describe her only job in life as being?

9. True or false: Angelica has more lines in Hamilton than Eliza does?

10. In which phrase used in a letter from Hamilton does Angelica spot a misplaced comma that changes the meaning?

11. Which city does Angelica sail off to when she leaves America?

12. She moves there with her husband, a man she describes as "someone who always..." what?

13. In the same breath, she notes her husband is not a lot of fun but that no one can match Alexander for... what?

14. What does Eliza recall Angelica told her she'd married in Hamilton, on reading about his indiscretions?

15. Where, as mentioned in the final number, is Angelica buried?

Answers on page 80

'Satisfied'

Alright, alright - give it up, for the Maid of Honour! How well do you know 'Satisfied'?

1. Which character speaks first to introduce Angelica in 'Satisfied'?

2. Who does Angelica toast first - the bride or the groom?

3. 'Satisfied' then moves into a rewind and flashback to which song that precedes it?

4. How many fundamental truths does Angelica realize at the exact same time?

5. Why does Angelica believe Hamilton is "after her"?

6. What does Angelica forget when Hamilton says "Hi"?

7. Aside from Hamilton, which other Founding Father is namechecked in 'Satisfied'?

8. How does Angelica describe Hamilton's beard?

9. And how does she describe his physique?

10. What is the first line we hear Hamilton deliver to Angelica in 'Satisfied'?

11. To which question from Angelica is Hamilton responding when he answers "Unimportant"?

12. Complete the quote. "I know my sister like I know my own..." *what*?

13. According to Angelica, you'll never find anyone as *what* or as *what* as Eliza?

14. What is it that Angelica says she sees when she fantasizes at night?

15. What number song is 'Satisfied' in the order of the show?

Answers on page 82

Whose Line Was It?

Can you remember who delivered these classic Hamilton lines?

1. "It's Ben Franklin with a key and a kite! You see it, right?"

2. "I have never been the type to try and grab the spotlight."

3. "I'm a trust fund, baby, you can trust me!"

4. "These are wise words, enterprising men quote 'em. Don't act surprised, you guys, 'cause I wrote 'em."

5. "I know you are a man of honor. I'm so sorry to bother you at home."

6. "Y'all look pretty good in ya' frocks. How 'bout when I get back, we all strip down to our socks?"

7. "Your sentences border on senseless. And you are paranoid in every paragraph."

8. "The plan is to fan this spark into a flame. But damn, it's getting dark, so let me spell out my name."

9. "We are engaged in a battle for our nation's very soul. Can you get us out of the mess we're in?"

10. "I wanna talk about what I have learned. The hard-won wisdom I have earned."

11. "My mother was a genius. My father commanded respect."

12. "Oceans rise, empires fall. We have seen each other through it all."

13. "I'm taking this horse by the reins. Making redcoats redder with bloodstains."

14. "I hope this letter finds you in good health, and in a prosperous enough position to put wealth in the pockets of people like me down on their luck."

15. "Look, when Britain taxed our tea, we got frisky. Imagine what gon' happen when you try to tax our whisky."

Answers on page 84

Burr

1. How long did it take Burr to graduate from college?

2. What year is it when Burr first meets Hamilton?

3. And what is Burr's "free advice" to Hamilton on their first meeting?

4. What, according to Burr, do rich folks love nothing more than to do?

5. What is the name of the woman with whom Burr is in love?

6. In which state is the British husband of Burr's love interest "trying to keep the colonies alive"?

7. True or false: Burr has the most lines in Hamilton?

8. Which one of the Schuyler sisters tells Burr that they disgust her?

9. In 'Schuyler Defeated', it is revealed Burr has switched allegiance to which political party?

10. In 'Wait For It', what does Burr describe his grandfather as?

11. Which general did Burr serve as a captain under, until that general "caught a bullet in the neck in Quebec"?

12. Against whom does Burr compete in 'The Election of 1800'?

13. What is the name of the town in which Hamilton and Burr's duel takes place?

14. What is the name of Burr's second in his duel with Hamilton?

15. Where does Burr say that his bullet strikes Hamilton?

Answers on page 86

Complete the Lyric

1. "Raise a glass to _____. Something they can never take away."

2. "How does a ragtag volunteer army in need of a _____ somehow defeat a global superpower?"

3. "I'm runnin' with the _____ _____ _____ and I am lovin' it! See, that's what happens when you up against the ruffians."

4. "Have you an ounce of regret? You accumulate _____, you accumulate power. Yet in their hour of need, you forget."

5. "I'm a diamond in the rough, a shiny piece of coal. Tryin' to reach my goal, my power of speech: _____."

6. "My name is Philip. I am a poet. I'm a little _____, but I can't show it."

7. "You and your words flooded my senses. Your sentences left me defenseless. You built me palaces out of _____."

8. "You say our love is _____ and you can't go on. You'll be the one complaining when I am gone."

9. "We will fight up close, seize the moment and stay in it. It's either that or meet the business end of a _____."

10. "A civics lesson from a slaver - hey neighbor, your debts are paid cause' you don't pay for labor."

11. "God help and forgive me, I wanna build something that's gonna _____ me."

12. "I'm just like my country. I'm young, _____, and hungry."

13. "Everything's legal in _____ _____."

14. "I am inimitable. I am an _____."

15. "_____...we get the job done."

Answers on page 88

George Washington

1. In 'Alexander Hamilton', how does Washington describe his relationship with Hamilton?

2. In 'Right Hand Man', Washington tells Hamilton that, in comparison to the British, their own military presence is "outgunned, outmanned, outnumbered" and what else?

3. In the same song, Washington refers to himself as the "venerated Virginian..." what?

4. Which term does Hamilton instruct Washington to stop calling him?

5. In which number does Washington tell Hamilton the story of how he led his men into a massacre when he took his first command?

6. In 'Right Hand Man', Washington is described as "the pride of..." where?

7. Which state does Washington tell Hamilton he is from?

8. Was Washington older or younger than Hamilton was when he took his first command?

9. What does Washington instruct Hamilton to draft after 'Cabinet Battle #2'?

10. According to George, what is "harder than winning"?

11. What type of tree does Washington tell Hamilton he wants to sit under?

12. In which song does Washington inform Hamilton of both Jefferson's resignation and his own intention to step down as president?

13. How many years does Washington say he has dedicated to his country "with an upright zeal", at the point he reveals his plan to step down?

14. True or false: Washington has no lines in 'Washington By Your Side'?

15. Who convinces Washington he needs his right hand man back?

Answers on page 90

Introductions

Can you tell the Hamilton character from their introduction?

1. "Ladies, I'm lookin' for a Mr..."

2. "Brrrah, brraaah, I am..."

3. "Daddy, Daddy, look! My name is..."

4. "Uh oh. But little does he know that his daughters..." [3 names]

5. "A month into this endeavor I receive a letter from a Mr..."

6. "Who's waitin' for me when I step in the place? My friend..."

7. "Pardon me, are you..."

8. "Showtime, showtime, yo! I'm..."

9. "What's your name, man?"

10. "Hear ye, hear ye, my name is…"

11. "Here comes the general."

12. "Someone's gotta keep the American promise, you simply must meet…"

13. "Oui oui, mon ami, je m'appelle…"

14. "Longing for Angelica, missing my wife. That's when…"

15. "And"

Answers on page 92

Last Lines

Can you name the Hamilton song by the last line?

1. "Figure it out, Alexander. That's an order from your commander."

2. "You're on your own."

3. "I can't stop till I get this plan through Congress."

4. "Nobody needs to know."

5. "They are going through the unimaginable."

6. "His poor wife."

7. "In New York you can be a new man."

8. "Daddy's calling."

9. "The world will never be the same, Alexander..."

10. "Burr, when you see Hamilton, thank him for the endorsement."

11. "Go home, Alexander. That's an order from your commander."

12. "Alexander, rumors only grow. And we both know what we know."

13. "Yeah, you'll blow us all away, someday, someday."

14. "President John Adams, good luck!"

15. "In the greatest city in the world!"

Answers on page 94

Lyrical Descriptions

Can you name the character by the description of them within Hamilton lyrics?

1. "A spy on the inside".

2. "An Icarus".

3. "A woman who has never been satisfied".

4. "The villain in your history".

5. "Mr. Age of Enlightenment".

6. "The latest graduate of King's College".

7. "The Princeton prodigy".

8. "That little guy who spoke to me".

9. "The oldest and the wittiest".

10. "America's favorite fighting Frenchman".

11. "Founder of the New York Post".

12. "The only man who can give us a command".

13. "Best of women".

14. "The tomcat".

15. "Red in the face".

Answers on page 96

Name the Song by the Lyric

1. "I'll write under a pseudonym, you'll see what I can do to him!"

2. "Awesome. Wow."

3. "Have you read this?"

4. "Someone in a rush next to someone lookin' pretty."

5. "Pride is not the word I'm looking for."

6. "Look, Grandpa's in the paper!"

7. "You told the whole world how you brought this girl into our bed."

8. "Freedom for America, Freedom for France!"

9. "The ship is in the harbor now, see if you can spot him."

10. "Don't call me son."

11. "No one has more resilience or matches my practical tactical brilliance!"

12. "Eliza, I don't have a dollar to my name."

13. "You don't have the votes."

14. "Sit down, John, you fat mother******!"

15. "My dog speaks more eloquently than thee."

<u>Answers on page 98</u>

Act Two

1. What is the first song of Act Two?

2. Which character MCs the two Cabinet Battles?

3. How much money does Hamilton give to Maria Reynolds on their first meeting?

4. Who succeeds George Washington as American president?

5. Which three characters are literally in the Room Where it Happens?

6. How old is Philip on the birthday on which he delivers his self-penned rap to Alexander?

7. Which two countries are on the verge of war when 'Cabinet Battle #2' is taking place?

8. Who fatally shoots Philip Hamilton in their duel?

9. Where does Philip make his duel challenge to that person?

10. Which character is described as a francophile?

11. 'Your Obedient Servant' is a song of correspondence between which two characters?

12. Which four people can Hamilton see watching him "from the other side" before he is struck by the bullet from Burr's gun?

13. Which river is Hamilton rowed back across after his duel with Burr?

14. Who lives longer, Eliza or Angelica?

15. What is the final song of Act Two?

Answers on page 100

Words That Rhyme With 'Burr'

Lin-Manuel Miranda has proved himself exceptional at rhyming words with Burr's surname. But which of the following does he actually use in Hamilton?

1. Bursar.

2. Sir.

3. Bird.

4. Mercer.

5. Sister.

6. Worst.

7. Nervous.

8. Fur.

9. Transfer.

10. Slur.

11. Sure.

12. Incur.

13. Concur.

14. Her.

15. Word.

Answers on page 102

Titles in Other Songs

Can you name the Hamilton song title that occurs in the lyrics of another Hamilton song?

1. "If I throw away _____, is this how you'll remember me? What if this bullet is my legacy?" - 'The World Was Wide Enough'.

2. "Then a _____ came and devastation reigned, our man saw his future drip, dripping down the drain." - 'Alexander Hamilton'.

3. "You've kept me from _____ for the last time." - 'Your Obedient Servant'.

4. "They are asking me to lead, I'm doing the best I can, to get the people that I need, I'm asking you to be my _____." - 'Non-Stop'.

5. "We'll pass it on to you, we'll give the world to you, and you'll _____." - 'Dear Theodosia'.

6. "The fact that you're alive is a miracle, just _____, that would be enough." - 'That Would Be Enough'.

7. "Oh, you get love for it, you get hate for it, you get nothing if you _____." - 'The Room Where It Happens'.

8. "But my God she looks so _____, and her body's saying 'hell yes'." - 'Say No to This'.

9. "And I'm never gonna stop until I make 'em, drop and _____ 'em up and scatter their remains." - 'Guns and Ships'.

10. "A winter's ball, and _____ are the envy of all." - 'A Winter's Ball'.

11. "As long as he can hold a pen, he's a threat. Let's let him know what _____" - 'The Adams Administration'.

12. "Let's _____ tonight, and then we'll teach them how to say goodbye." - 'One Last Time'.

13. "Let me tell you what I wish I'd known, when I was young and dreamed of glory, you have no control, _____." - 'History Has Its Eyes on You'.

14. "I know I don't deserve you, Eliza, but hear me out, _____." - 'It's Quiet Uptown'.

15. "I'm _____ I'm at your service, sir. I have been looking for you." - 'Aaron Burr, Sir'.

Answers on page 104

Thomas Jefferson

1. What is Jefferson's role announced as when he first appears in Hamilton?

2. What is the name of Jefferson's home, to which he returns ("I gotta be in...") after helping Lafayette to draft a declaration?

3. Who does Jefferson ask to open his letter from the president?

4. What role does Jefferson take in the Washington administration?

5. Which state are Jefferson and James Madison both from?

6. What color does Jefferson mainly wear in Hamilton?

7. Which Macbeth character does Hamilton describe Jefferson as in 'Take a Break'?

8. Does Jefferson become the second, third or fourth American president?

9. In described his role in 'The Room Where It Happens', Jefferson says that he arranged the meeting, the menu, the venue and what else?

10. What does Jefferson describe Hamilton's dress sense as being like, in Cabinet Battle #2?

11. What does Jefferson answer when Hamilton says "I have been fighting for the South alone. Where have you been?"

12. In which song does Jefferson decide to tender his resignation as Secretary of State?

13. According to Jefferson in 'Cabinet Battle #2', who is leading the French following King Louis XVI's execution?

14. Who does Jefferson beat in the 1800 election to become president?

15. What creation of Hamilton's does Jefferson (reluctantly) admit is a work of genius?

Answers on page 106

Quickfire Trios

Can you name these trios of characters (who all have singing parts) from Hamilton?

Past/Present/Future Presidents

1. _____ _____.

2. _____ _____.

3. _____ _____.

Schuyler Sisters

4. _____ _____.

5. _____ _____.

6. _____ _____.

Duel Winners

7. _____ _____.

8. _____ _____.

9. _____ _____.

Duel Losers

10. _____ _____.

11. _____ _____.

12. _____ _____.

The Four of Us (minus Hamilton)

13. _____ _____.

14. _____ _____.

15. _____ _____.

Answers on page 108

Answers on page 108

Historical Factcheck

Because, sometimes, a writer has to take a little creative licence.

1. Phillip Schuyler is shown to have only three children. How many did he actually have?

2. The musical shows George Eacker cheating by shooting Philip on the count of seven in their duel. When did he actually fire?

3. Laurens is noted to drink Sam Adams beer in 'The Story of Tonight'. In which century was this brand actually created?

4. Angelica is shown to marry after she moved away from Hamilton, but she actually married John Barker Church three years before she even met Hamilton. How many children did she have with him by the time she met Hamilton for real?

5. We see Hamilton mourning the death of his son Philip when he promotes Jefferson to break the stalemate in the 1800 election. In reality, which year did Philip's duel and death occur?

6. Hamilton portrays the Ten Duel Commandments a few times in the show. How many duel commandments were there actually?

7. Madison, Burr and Jefferson were not present in the real-life meeting in which Hamilton admitted to his affair with Maria Reynolds. Which eventual president is said to have actually led the meeting and leaked Hamilton's affair?

8. In the musical, Alexander is shown to be the first of Laurens, Mulligan, Lafayette and himself to get married. In reality, which of them got married before he did?

9. On stage, Burr and Hamilton's duel occurs in the aftermath of Burr losing his race for the American presidency in 1800. However their rivalry actually came to a head in 1804 when Hamilton publicly derided Burr while he ran for which other political role?

10. In 'Take a Break', a nine-year-old Philip says "I have a sister, but I want a little brother." How many younger brothers did Philip have by the age of nine?

11. Hamilton was never actually fired by John Adams; instead he actually resigned from office, but which president was he serving under at the time?

12. John Jay didn't actually write five *Federalist Papers* before he got sick. How many did he manage?

13. Eliza was rarely known as such. By which two variations of her name was she more commonly referred to?

14. It's not shown in Hamilton but Jefferson had a running mate in the 1800 election. Who was it?

15. Philip's death is shown to bring Hamilton and Eliza back together after The Reynolds Pamphlet, though certain events in the timeline show this is unlikely. How many children did they have together between The Reynolds Pamphlet coming out and Philip's death?

Answers on page 110

Anagrams

Can you unscramble the names of these Hamilton people or things that featured in the musical?

1. Journal Hens.

2. Casually Cheering.

3. Urban Roar.

4. Masculine Leg Hurl.

5. Generating Go Show.

6. Eggcup Shy Lyre.

7. Hazily Recluse.

8. Almond Jerseys.

9. Mainland Latex Hero.

10. Geek Gringo.

11. Ammo Jade Sins.

12. Daily Ransomer.

13. Anatomize Hill.

14. Horseman Jets Off.

15. A Fatty Eel.

Answers on page 112

Original Broadway Cast

A round all about the original Broadway cast of Hamilton.

1. Who played Alexander Hamilton?

2. Who played Eliza Hamilton (née Schuyler)?

3. Who played Aaron Burr?

4. Who played Angelica Schuyler?

5. Who played Lafayette?

6. Who played George Washington?

7. Who played Maria Reynolds?

8. Who played Hercules Mulligan?

9. Who played Thomas Jefferson?

10. Who played John Laurens?

11. Who played King George?

12. Who played Peggy Schuyler?

13. Who played James Madison?

14. Who played Philip Hamilton?

15. Which three members of the original Broadway cast also played their roles in the workshop production at the Vassar Reading Festival in 2013?

Answers on page 114

Tiebreakers

Tied at the end of your quiz? Here's some "closest to" questions to help separate the wheat from the chaff.

1. In which year was Lin-Manuel Miranda born?

2. In which year did the real Alexander Hamilton die?

3. As of 2020, Hamilton holds the record for most Tony Award nominations. How many did it receive?

4. How many Tony awards did Hamilton win?

5. How many different fronts does Hamilton estimate that Jefferson and he have fought over?

6. How many essays did Hamilton and co. originally intend to write to defend the new United States Constitution?

7. And how many essays did they actually write?

8. In which year is 'A Winter's Ball' set?

9. And in which year does 'Yorktown' take place?

10. How old was Hamilton when "a hurricane destroyed [his] hometown"?

11. In 'My Shot', what age does Hamilton say he used to believe he wouldn't live past?

12. To the nearest whole minute, for how long does King George appear on stage in Hamilton?

13. To the nearest hundred, how many lines does Alexander Hamilton have in Hamilton?

14. To the nearest whole minute, how long does the cast soundtrack of the musical last for?

15. In which year are Alexander Hamilton and Aaron Burr shown to meet?

Answers on page 116

ANSWERS

Answer Sheet: General Knowledge

1. "An American Musical".

2. Angelica Schuyler.

3. John Laurens.

4. The Reynolds Pamphlet.

5. King George III.

6. 'Dear Theodosia'.

7. Tailor. That's probably why his pants looked hot.

8. *The Federalist Papers*.

9. Mercer. (And all he had to do was die.)

10. $1,000.

11. Virginia.

12. 10.

13. 'The World Turned Upside Down'.

14. Thomas Jefferson. You know why? Because he was the president.

15. "Who tells your story?"

Answer Sheet: Hamilton

1. Fourteen.

2. King's College (now Columbia University).

3. The ten dollar bill.

4. A whore and a Scotsman.

5. Martha Washington.

6. Scholar.

7. 51.

8. Secretary of State.

9. A million.

10. Burr, in 'The World Was Wide Enough'.

11. The Coast Guard.

12. Princeton.

13. The new U.S. Constitution.

14. Nathaniel Pendleton.

15. "Alexander Hamilton."

Answer Sheet: The Nerd Round

1. Ron Chernow.

2. The Hamilton Mixtape.

3. The Richard Rodgers Theatre. It's also where Lin-Manuel Miranda debuted *In the Heights*.

4. Non-Stop, appropriately, at 6:25.

5. Hugh Laurie.

6. Karen Olivo, of *In the Heights* fame.

7. Levi Weeks.

8. 'Tomorrow There'll Be More of Us'.

9. Guns and Ships, in which Lafayette spits 19 words in the space of 3 seconds. (That's 6.333333 words per second.)

10. *Curb Your Enthusiasm*.

11. Burr. "I feel an equal affinity with Burr," he told *The New Yorker*.

12. 'Ya Boy Is Killing 'Em'. Miranda decided it was too on-the-nose.

13. Philip Schuyler.

14. *Parks and Recreation*. "Such a Leslie Knope thing to do."

15. "Raise a glass to freedom..."

Answer Sheet: The Ten Duel Commandments

1. "Satisfaction".

2. "Apologize".

3. "Second".

4. "Lieutenant".

5. "Peace".

6. "Shoots".

7. "Pistols".

8. "Deniability".

9. "Dry".

10. "Note".

11. "Hell".

12. "Adrenaline".

13. "Negotiate".

14. "Courage".

15. "Fire".

Answer Sheet: Eliza

1. Green.

2. New York.

3. One week.

4. Harlem.

5. Piano.

6. "Be true."

7. John Adams.

8. 'That Would Be Enough'.

9. Philip.

10. 'Burn'.

11. 'Who Lives, Who Dies, Who Tells Your Story'.

12. Wives and women.

13. 50 years.

14. The Washington Monument.

15. Private orphanage.

Answer Sheet: Act One

1. Aaron Burr.

2. Lancelot.

3. Pints of Sam Adams.

4. "Seven feet ahead of me?"

5. 32,000.

6. Cannons.

7. Thomas Jefferson and James Madison. You might think it's Lafayette and Hercules Mulligan, but there's no French accent there.

8. Charles Lee.

9. Their horses.

10. Their reliability with the ladies.

11. South Carolina, his home state.

12. James Madison and John Jay.

13. "Rochambeau".

14. Chesapeake Bay.

15. 'Non-Stop'.

Answer Sheet: Follow That Line

1. "What'll you fall for?"

2. "Yo, this one's mine."

3. "I'm young, scrappy and hungry."

4. "They all look small."

5. "Angelica tried to take a bite of me."

6. "To remind you of my love."

7. "John Adams doesn't have a real job anyway."

8. "Most disputes die and no one shoots."

9. "At least I keep his eyes in my life."

10. "Between the sinners and the saints."

11. "You have your mother's name."

12. "Include women in the sequel."

13. "Uh, do whatever you want - I'm super dead."

14. "Diametrically opposed foes."

15. "You can't put it out from inside the house."

Answer Sheet: Angelica

1. Pink.

2. "Common Sense" by Thomas Paine.

3. "A mind at work".

4. "Like your daddy's got money."

5. Macbeth.

6. Insidious.

7. Lafayette.

8. "To marry rich".

9. False. Angelica has 246. Eliza has 324.

10. "My dearest, Angelica".

11. London.

12. "Pays".

13. Turn of phrase.

14. An Icarus.

15. Trinity Church.

Answer Sheet: 'Satisfied'

1. John Laurens.

2. The groom.

3. 'Helpless'.

4. Three.

5. Because she is a Schuyler sister. That elevates his status.

6. Her dang name.

7. Benjamin Franklin.

8. "Peach fuzz... and he can't even grow it!"

9. "A hunger-panged frame".

10. "You strike me as a woman who has never been satisfied." Direct.

11. "Where's your family from?"

12. "Mind".

13. "You will never find anyone as trusting or as kind."

14. Alexander's eyes.

15. It is the 11th song.

Answer Sheet: Whose Line Was It?

1. Angelica.

2. Eliza.

3. Burr.

4. Jefferson.

5. Maria Reynolds.

6. Philip.

7. Eliza.

8. Alexander.

9. James Madison.

10. George Washington.

11. Burr.

12. King George.

13. Lafayette.

14. James Reynolds.

15. Jefferson.

Answer Sheet: Burr

1. Two years.

2. 1776.

3. "Talk less, smile more."

4. "Going downtown and slummin' it with the poor."

5. Theodosia.

6. Georgia.

7. False. He comes in second place with 655, some distance behind Hamilton himself.

8. Angelica. Ah, so she's discussed him.

9. The Democratic-Republican party.

10. "A fire-and-brimstone preacher".

11. General Montgomery.

12. Thomas Jefferson.

13. Weehawken.

14. William P. Van Ness.

15. "Right between his ribs".

Answer Sheet: Complete the Lyric

1. "Freedom" - 'The Story of Tonight'.

2. "Shower" - 'Guns and Ships'.

3. "Sons of Liberty" - 'Yorktown'.

4. "Debt" - 'Cabinet Battle #2'.

5. "Unimpeachable" - 'My Shot'.

6. "Nervous" - 'Blow Us All Away'.

7. "Paragraphs" - 'Burn'.

8. "Draining" - 'You'll Be Back'.

9. "Bayonet" - 'Yorktown'.

10. "Slaver" - 'Cabinet Battle #1'.

11. "Outlive" - 'The Room Where It Happens'.

12. "Scrappy" - 'My Shot'.

13. "New Jersey" - 'Blow Us All Away'.

14. "Original" - 'Wait For It'.

15. "Immigrants" - 'Yorktown'.

Answer Sheet: George Washington

1. "Me? I trusted him."

2. "Outplanned".

3. "Veteran".

4. "Son".

5. 'History Has Its Eyes On You'.

6. Mount Vernon.

7. Virginia.

8. Younger.

9. "A statement of neutrality".

10. Governing.

11. "My own vine and fig tree".

12. 'One Last Time'.

13. 45.

14. True. He briefly appears on stage for Jefferson to hand him his letter of resignation.

15. Lafayette.

Answer Sheet: Introductions

1. George Eacker.

2. Hercules Mulligan.

3. Philip Hamilton.

4. Angelica, Eliza and Peggy.

5. James Reynolds.

6. James Madison.

7. Aaron Burr. (Sir.)

8. John Laurens.

9. Alexander Hamilton.

10. Samuel Seabury.

11. George Washington.

12. Thomas Jefferson.

13. Lafayette.

14. Maria Reynolds.

15. Peggy Schuyler.

Answer Sheet: Last Lines

1. 'Cabinet Battle #1'.

2. 'What Comes Next?'.

3. 'Take a Break'.

4. 'Say No to This'.

5. 'It's Quiet Uptown'.

6. 'The Reynolds Pamphlet'.

7. 'Helpless'.

8. 'Cabinet Battle #2'.

9. 'Guns and Ships'.

10. 'The Election of 1800'.

11. 'Meet Me Inside'.

12. 'We Know'.

13. 'Dear Theodosia'.

14. 'I Know Him'.

15. 'The Schuyler Sisters'.

Answer Sheet: Lyrical Descriptions

1. Hercules Mulligan.

2. Alexander Hamilton.

3. Angelica Schuyler.

4. Aaron Burr.

5. Thomas Jefferson.

6. Philip Hamilton.

7. Aaron Burr.

8. John Adams.

9. Angelica Schuyler.

10. Lafayette.

11. Alexander Hamilton.

12. George Washington.

13. Eliza Schuyler Hamilton.

14. Alexander Hamilton.

15. James Madison.

Answer Sheet: Name the Song by the Lyric

1. 'One Last Time'.

2. 'What Comes Next?'

3. 'The Reynolds Pamphlet'.

4. 'The Schuyler Sisters'.

5. 'Dear Theodosia'.

6. 'Schuyler Defeated'.

7. 'Burn'.

8. 'Yorktown'.

9. 'Alexander Hamilton'.

10. 'Meet Me Inside'.

11. 'Guns and Ships'.

12. 'Helpless'.

13. 'Cabinet Battle #1'.

14. 'The Adams Administration'.

15. 'Farmer Refuted'.

Answer Sheet: Act Two

1. 'What'd I Miss?'

2. George Washington.

3. $30. ("I gave her 30 bucks that I had socked away.")

4. John Adams.

5. Hamilton, Thomas Jefferson and James Madison. "Two Virginians and an immigrant walk into a bar..."

6. Nine.

7. England and France.

8. George Eacker.

9. A theater on Broadway.

10. Thomas Jefferson. (At least they know he knows where France is.)

11. Hamilton and Burr.

12. John Laurens, his son Philip, his mother and George Washington.

13. The Hudson River.

14. Eliza.

15. 'Who Lives, Who Dies, Who Tells Your Story'.

Answer Sheet: Words That Rhyme With 'Burr'

1. True.

2. True.

3. False.

4. True.

5. True.

6. True.

7. True.

8. False.

9. False.

10. False.

11. True.

12. False.

13. False.

14. True.

15. True.

Answer Sheet: Titles in Other Songs

1. 'My Shot'.

2. 'Hurricane'.

3. 'The Room Where It Happens'.

4. 'Right Hand Man'.

5. 'Blow Us All Away'.

6. 'Stay Alive'.

7. 'Wait For It'.

8. 'Helpless'.

9. 'Burn'.

10. 'The Schuyler Sisters'.

11. 'We Know'.

12. 'Take a Break'.

13. 'Who Lives, Who Dies, Who Tells Your Story'.

14. 'That Would Be Enough'.

15. 'Alexander Hamilton'.

Answer Sheet: Thomas Jefferson

1. Ambassador to France.

2. Monticello.

3. Sally.

4. Secretary of State. (Great.)

5. Virginia.

6. Purple. (He's modelled after Prince.)

7. Macduff.

8. Third.

9. The seating.

10. "Fake royalty".

11. "France".

12. 'Washington On Your Side'.

13. "The people".

14. Aaron Burr.

15. Hamilton's financial system.

Answer Sheet: Quickfire Trios

Past/Present/Future Presidents

1. George Washington.

2. Thomas Jefferson.

3. James Madison.

Schuyler Sisters

4. Angelica Schuyler.

5. Elizabeth Schuyler.

6. Peggy Schuyler.

Duel Winners

7. John Laurens.

8. George Eacker.

9. Aaron Burr.

Duel Losers

10. Charles Lee.

11. Philip Hamilton.

12. Alexander Hamilton.

The Four of Us (minus Hamilton)

13. John Laurens.

14. Hercules Mulligan.

15. Lafayette.

Answer Sheet: Historical Factcheck

1. 15, including two sons who survived to adulthood, despite Angelica's line in 'Satisfied'.

2. Reportedly, a few minutes after the count of ten, and only then when he mistook Philip raising his gun to the sky as an attempt to shoot him.

3. The 20th.

4. Two.

5. 1801.

6. 25.

7. James Monroe.

8. All of them.

9. Governor of New York.

10. Two.

11. Washington. Although Hamilton co-wrote Washington's farewell address, he wasn't in the cabinet anymore, having resigned two years earlier.

12. Four. (Although he wrote the fifth after he recovered, so this is a very pedantic point.)

13. Elizabeth and Betsy.

14. Burr. Burr wasn't originally running against Jefferson; he was running for Vice President. But then a number of people decided they preferred him to Jefferson. Then Hamilton endorsed the latter.

15. Two.

Answer Sheet: Anagrams

1. Journal Hens = John Laurens.

2. Casually Cheering = Angelica Schuyler.

3. Urban Roar = Aaron Burr.

4. Masculine Leg Hurl = Hercules Mulligan.

5. Generating Go Show = George Washington.

6. Eggcup Shy Lyre = Peggy Schuyler.

7. Hazily Recluse = Eliza Schuyler.

8. Almond Jerseys = James Reynolds.

9. Mainland Latex Hero = Alexander Hamilton.

10. Geek Gringo = King George.

11. Ammo Jade Sins = James Madison.

12. Daily Ransomer = Maria Reynolds.

13. Anatomize Hill = Eliza Hamilton.

14. Horseman Jets Off = Thomas Jefferson.

15. A Fatty Eel = Lafayette.

Answer Sheet: Original Broadway Cast

1. Lin-Manuel Miranda.

2. Phillipa Soo.

3. Leslie Odom Jr.

4. Renée Elise Goldsberry.

5. Daveed Diggs.

6. Christopher Jackson.

7. Jasmine Cephas Jones.

8. Okieriete Onaodowan.

9. Daveed Diggs.

10. Anthony Ramos.

11. Jonathan Groff.

12. Jasmine Cephas Jones.

13. Okieriete Onaodowan.

14. Anthony Ramos.

15. Lin-Manuel Miranda, Daveed Diggs and Christopher Jackson.

Answer Sheet: Tiebreakers

1. 1980.

2. 1804.

3. 16. (Although some were in the same category, so it could only have won 13.)

4. 11.

5. 75.

6. 25.

7. 85.

8. 1780.

9. 1781.

10. 17.

11. 20.

12. Nine minutes.

13. 900. 916 to be precise.

14. 2 hours, 23 minutes.

15. 1776.

Printed in Poland
by Amazon Fulfillment
Poland Sp. z o.o., Wrocław

63667547R00070